Creepy Crawlies

CONTENTS

Translated from the Italian by Maureen Spurgeon

Brown Watson

ENGLAND

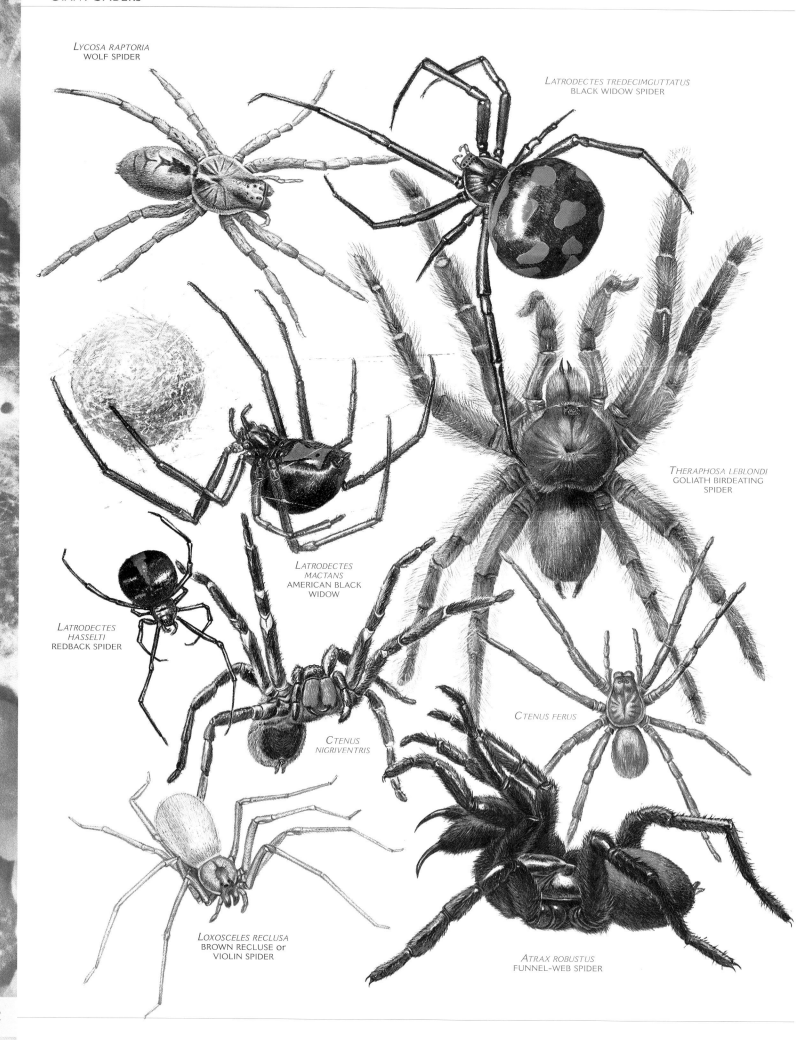

LYCOSA RAPTORIA
WOLF SPIDER

LATRODECTES TREDECIMGUTTATUS
BLACK WIDOW SPIDER

THERAPHOSA LEBLONDI
GOLIATH BIRDEATING
SPIDER

LATRODECTES
MACTANS
AMERICAN BLACK
WIDOW

LATRODECTES
HASSELTI
REDBACK SPIDER

CTENUS
NIGRIVENTRIS

CTENUS FERUS

LOXOSCELES RECLUSA
BROWN RECLUSE or
VIOLIN SPIDER

ATRAX ROBUSTUS
FUNNEL-WEB SPIDER

BLACK WIDOW SPIDER

Habitat: low plants, stones, corners or walls

Web: ragged, irregular

Length: about 15 mm

Poison: deadly

Most spiders in the class **Latrodectes** are generally small, but poisonous – such as The Black Widow spider. There are six species of Black Widow. The most common lives in the area of the Mediterranean and all very hot zones.

Although it is only 10-15 mm long, this spider is always hungry and is much-feared. It has a poisonous bite which can produce pain, sickness and temporary breathing problems. The bite, however, is rarely fatal to humans.

The female spider looks more frightening than the male, both in size and appearance, with her abdomen usually adorned with blood red spots. She hides among stones and bushes and spins a web made with threads of silk from the top of her body, abdomen turned upwards.

The Black Widow will not hesitate to attack animals larger than itself and grasshoppers are among its favourite prey. The female builds a clear-coloured, sphere-shaped cocoon, where she lays her eggs. The spider gets the name of Black Widow due to the female's habit of eating the much smaller male after mating.

Díd you know...

The **spider** usually has 8 eyes, but those which live in caves have none. The average length of the body is 2 cm, but some tropical species, such as the bird-eating Mygale, measure 9 cm and with the legs can even be more than 20 cm!

The **Tarantula** belongs to the class Lycosa. According to popular belief, its bite can cause a sort of frenzy which can lead to death. In fact, its bite is not very dangerous.

The male of the **Black Widow** wraps its sperm in a soft net which it takes to the female to fertilize her eggs.

Closely related to the European Black Widow is the famous **American Black Widow**, Latrodectes mactans.

The **Theraphosa leblondi** (Goliath Birdeating Spider) is from South America. At the approach of an enemy, it tears into the skin with its rear claws to confuse its victim, causing strong skin irritation.

Living in temperate regions are two spiders of the genus **Ctenus**, both very poisonous.

Another spider much feared because of its poisonous bite is the **Atrax** (Funnel-Web Spider) widespread in tropical regions.

LYCOSA

Habitat: ground

Web: underground covering

Length of body: about 25 mm

Length of legs: 25 mm

Poison: almost harmless

There are many species of **lycosa**, spiders of small or medium size, which are distinguished by their home. Whilst other spiders make a web, a lycosa species finds a hole in the ground which it lines with a soft web of silk, to make it a comfortable underground sleeve, and which it can then close with a little silk cover. The cover opens or closes the entrance of the hole, making it into a trap. Each hole is inhabited by a solitary female; the male just keeps watch and goes in search of a mate only during the mating period, then flees before being eaten by his mate.

One species of lycosa is called the Ground Spider, or Wolf Spider because of its aggressive nature. The Wolf Spider runs fast across ground in search of prey, especially at night. It identifies its prey with the help of three rows of eyes – two medium-sized eyes in the top row, two large eyes in the middle row, and four small eyes in the bottom row.

MORE ABOUT SPIDERS

DEVELOPMENT, DISTRIBUTION AND HABITAT

The oldest forms of arachnids began a hundred million years ago with creatures similar to today's scorpions. Today, there are arachnids almost all over the world, mostly in very hot, damp regions. But some live in countries with temperate climates, and there are species of spiders which can be found within the Arctic Circle.

NUTRITION

Arachnids are meat-eaters and fearsome predators. For instance – a scorpion feeds on live prey, such as beetles and cockroaches, which it tears with its claws then sucks out the edible parts. The spider covers its prey with its gastric juices to 'melt' it before sucking the remains into its mouth.

The **Salticus sanguinolentus** (Jumping Spider, see bottom left) has eight eyes arranged in three rows; those in the middle are larger than the others and work rather like the telephoto lens of a camera. This gives the spider an enlarged image of its prey, but with a limited range. So, this spider must move in quickly before hurling itself on its victim.

Almost all spiders can spin thread. The common and harmless house spider spins its thread into a web and lives in the thickest part.

The web of the **Micrathena** (Orb Web Spider) is much more intricate. With its plated, spiny abdomen, this is a spider typical of those living in hot countries.

COMMON CHARACTERISTICS

The body of an arachnid is divided into a front part and a back part (the cephalothorax and the abdomen). Arachnids do not have antennae; the first pair of appendages are formed either like a hook or as pincers which the arachnid uses to grab, grind up and then put the food in its mouth.

BEHAVIOUR

All arachnids are aggressive creatures, ready to attack and to conquer their prey.
The scorpion uses its poisonous sting to kill. Spiders are experts in making soft webs, transparent and sticky, to trap their prey. An adult Daddy Long-Legs has a pair of glands which secrete an evil-smelling liquid.

Land dwelling creatures

We know of around 36,000 species of arachnid, but many thousands more exist. Most live on the land although a few are aquatic.

All arachnids have the same type of body, in two distinct parts – a **cephalothorax** or a prosoma (head and thorax fused together) protected on the back by a rigid cover called the **carapace**, and six pairs of jointed appendages – a pair of **chelicerae**, one of **pedipalps** and four pairs of jointed claws – and an abdomen or **opisthosoma**, which has no appendages. The pincer-like chelicerae, nearest the mouth, are also used to grip, for the injection of poison, as well as for spinning silk.

Photograph: above, Crab Spider. Facing page: top right, a Sac Spider.

The **pedipalps** can have various forms and functions; sometimes they are used for chewing, sometimes as huge, powerful pincers, as organs of reproduction, for taste and for gripping. The fourth pair of claws are for moving, digging, swimming, for **winding silk** and catching prey.

Scorpions, spiders and some mites have **poisonous glands**. Spiders and some other arachnids have spinning glands. Breathing organs are tubular trachea or lungs. In many mites, breathing is through the skin. Males and females are often quite different, as is the case with spiders.

Reproduction is by laying eggs, rarely oviparous (where eggs are hatched in the body of the female before the young emerge).

Arachnids belong to the sub phylum of Chelicerates (animals with pincers) and are divided into many types.

Scorpions have two large pedipalps which end in pincers and a tail with a poisonous sting.

Psuedoscorpions (also called false scorpions) are very small (from 1–8 mm) and without a tail. **Solifugae** (sun spiders) are large in size, covered with a thick fur and with two large claws shaped like pincers. **Uropygi** are nocturnal. They live in damp, tropical and sub-tropical regions. **Amblypygi** have small, flat bodies with very long, spiny pedipalps. **Spiders** are the most numerous of all arachnids. There are over 26,000 known species.

The **Opiliones** (Daddy Long-Legs) have small bodies and very long legs. They live in temperate and tropical regions. Most mites are parasites, living off plant material or other animals. They are widespread on the ground and in both the sea and fresh water.

ITALIAN SCORPION

Reproduction: oviparous

Habitat: warm, damp places, from the plains to the mountains

Length: 3.5-5.5 cm

This scorpion belongs to a family with more than 60 species spread throughout all the continents with the exception of Australia and Africa, south of the Sahara Desert.

There are four species of Italian Scorpion. It is an animal with mainly nocturnal habits and it flees from daylight, sheltering in cracks and clefts in walls. It feeds on insects and frogs which it catches with its claws and kills with its nippers or with the deadly sting in its tail. The Italian Scorpion has poor sight and so it has to wait until its victim is within range until it can capture it.

The female carries her young on her back for a few weeks after they are born. The young scorpions can only move about after their first moulting (shedding of their skin covering). Then, if they cannot flee fast enough, they are usually eaten by their mother, who mistakes them for prey. Scorpions can reproduce when they are about 3 or 4 years old. The young are very pale and are also different to the adult in size and proportion, because the body is more stocky. In addition, they have no hairs on their legs and no talons at the tips of their claws.

Did you know...

Scorpions have a highly developed sense of touch. This compensates for their sight, which is so poor that they cannot even see their prey until it is just a short distance away, nor can they chase it if it flees from attack.

It is sometimes believed that if a **scorpion** is surrounded by fire, it will die by stinging itself. The truth is probably that the scorpion stings itself by accident, contorted by the fear of the fire and the pain of burning.

The poison of the **African Yellow Fattail Scorpion** is very powerful. It can kill a dog in a few seconds and cause serious harm to a human being!

The **Yellow-Tail Scorpion** gets its name due to the colour of its poisonous tail. It is one of the scorpions which can be found in parts of Europe. Its sting is not dangerous to humans.

Among the largest scorpions found in Europe, is the **Iurus Dufourensis**.

The **Desert Hairy Scorpion** is common in the hot regions of the southern USA and South America. Its colouring is easily confused with the sandy surroundings where it lives.

The **Flat Back Scorpion** and the **Florida Rock Scorpion** are two other American species. The sting of the **Florida Bark Scorpion** has been known to cause many deaths.

IMPERIAL SCORPION

Reproduction: ovoviparous

Habitat: hot, damp forest regions

Length: 15-18 cm

This large scorpion lives in the hot, damp forests of central Africa. It is a nocturnal animal, hunting for invertebrates, lizards and small mammals under the cover of darkness and which it catches with its front claws and then stings again and again. After that, scorpion takes its victim to its lair, tearing it to shreds with its claws before eating it.

During mating time, the male approaches the female with caution, in case she mistakes him for prey. Then, when the male is sure that he is 'recognized', he begins courting her, catching her claws in his and beginning a sort of dance. The purpose of this dance is for the male to find a suitable place to deposit his spermatophore, containing his fertile sperm, and then position the female over this so that the eggs which she lays will be fertilized. This dance can last hours or up to two days. Some months after, the young scorpions are born.

CENTRUROIDES GRACILIS
FLORIDA BARK SCORPION

PANDINUS IMPERATOR
EMPEROR SCORPION

HADRURUS ARIZONENSIS
DESERT HAIRY SCORPION

EUSCORPIUS ITALICUS
ITALIAN SCORPION

HADOGENES BICOLOR
FLAT ROCK SCORPION

ANDROCTONUS AUSTRALIS
YELLOW FATTAIL SCORPION

IURUS DUFOURENSIS

EUSCORPIUS FLAVICAUDUS
YELLOW-TAIL SCORPION

Did you know...

The gigantic **Mastigoproctus giganteus** belongs to the **Uropygi** order. It is about 7 cm long and lives in Mexico and in the southern United States. Despite its menacing appearance and its hunger for catching frogs and small toads, it is harmless to humans.

The **Prynichus reniformis** moves on three pairs of legs, walking sideways, whilst using its long, spiny **pedipalps** as a trap for catching insects and large cockroaches. The first pair of legs, long and soft, function as organs for touch.

The **Phalangim opilio** (Daddy Long-Legs) has only two eyes. It does not spin silk and the male is almost identical to the female. It risks losing at least one of its thread-like legs when it has to flee from danger. Unlike spiders, the lost leg does not grow again.

Among other species of **Opiliones** we find the **Ischyropsalis hellwig**, with its huge pincers.

The **Galeodes arabs** is a large nocturnal arachnid of the order of **Solifugae** living in Europe and Asia; with its highly-developed pincers it can catch and eat termites, lizards and small mammals.

There are thousands of species of **mites**, all very tiny and which live at all latitudes and altitudes (up to 5500m). They are very resistant parasites which feed on plants and animals, such as the Sheep Tick and Castor Bean Tick.

CASTOR BEAN TICK

Habitat: animal parasite

Length: about 15 mm

The Castor Bean Tick may not seem very interesting. But, this tiny mite can be a very dangerous enemy both for animals and humans.

Like many mites, the Castor Bean Tick can transmit many disease-carrying viruses, some of which can cause death. That is why it can be very dangerous to touch or even to go near certain types of ticks. One bite can have terrible consequences.

The tick feeds on the blood of whatever creature it lives on, sucking through a beak formed by the claws of its pedipalps. It draws out the liquid by pumping movements of the stomach.

The life cycle of the tick is simple. The innocent-looking larva climbs a blade of grass, then waits for an animal to come along on to which it can move. After various moultings, it reaches the adult phase. Then it mates on its host plant or animal and the female falls to the ground to lay her eggs and then die. The new-born ticks will continue the life cycle.

PSEUDOSCORPIONS: BOOK SCORPION

Habitat: fields, libraries

Length: just a few millimetres

There are more than 1500 species of pseudoscorpions which live in all hot and temperate regions throughout the world. They are related to scorpions, but they do not have a poisonous sting and the body is not so long.

All pseudoscorpions are small, no more than a few millimetres. They are lively little creatures which live in cracks, beneath sacks and under the bark of trees, in rotting material, in nests of small mammals and in the honeycomb of bees. One of the most widespread is the Book Scorpion. This is a harmless creature which lives in the pages of books or among powdery paper, in libraries or in old, damp documents. The favourite prey of the **pseudoscorpion** are insects, especially the small, wingless insect, the collembolan. Unlike the spider and the scorpion, the pseudoscorpion is not limited to sucking or eating the soft parts of their prey, they eat everything. Sometimes, they attach themselves to ants or to scorpions to be carried along.

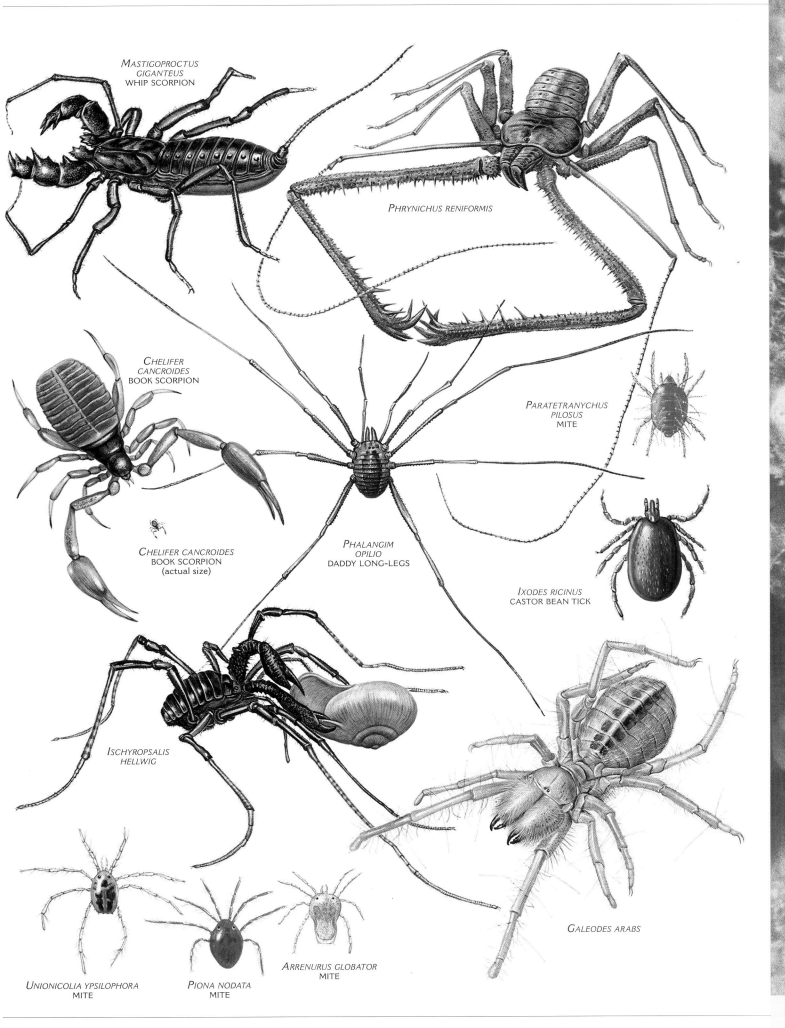

MASTIGOPROCTUS
GIGANTEUS
WHIP SCORPION

PHRYNICHUS RENIFORMIS

CHELIFER
CANCROIDES
BOOK SCORPION

PARATETRANYCHUS
PILOSUS
MITE

CHELIFER CANCROIDES
BOOK SCORPION
(actual size)

PHALANGIM
OPILIO
DADDY LONG-LEGS

IXODES RICINUS
CASTOR BEAN TICK

ISCHYROPSALIS
HELLWIG

UNIONICOLIA YPSILOPHORA
MITE

PIONA NODATA
MITE

ARRENURUS GLOBATOR
MITE

GALEODES ARABS

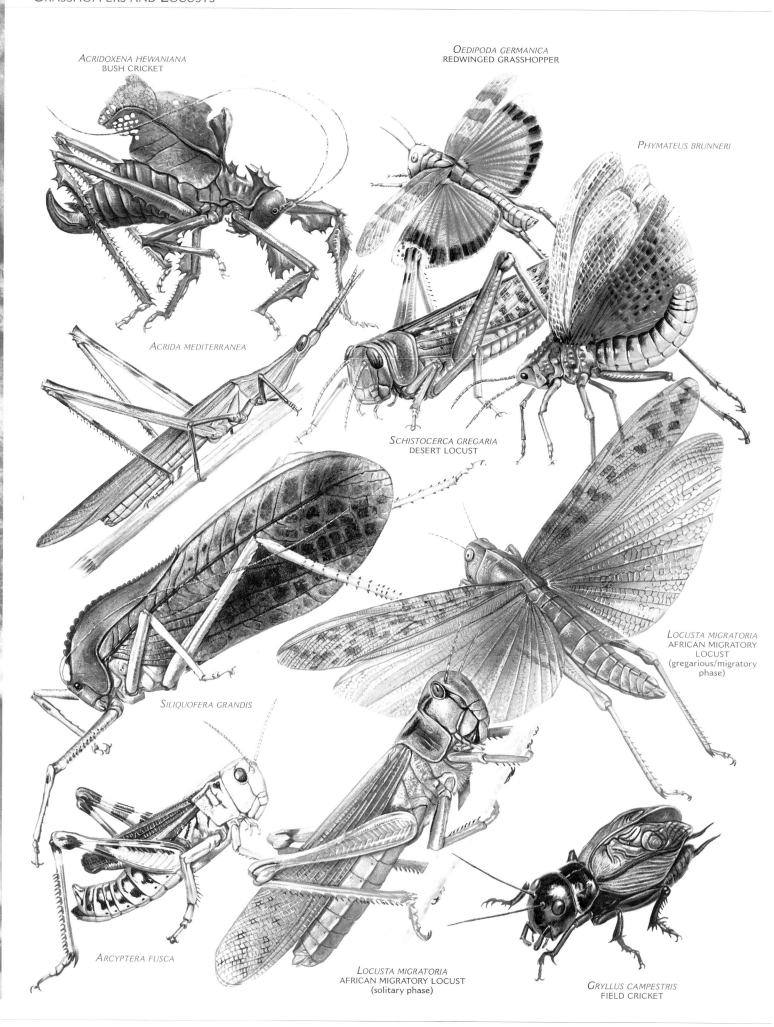

ACRIDOXENA HEWANIANA
BUSH CRICKET

OEDIPODA GERMANICA
REDWINGED GRASSHOPPER

PHYMATEUS BRUNNERI

ACRIDA MEDITERRANEA

SCHISTOCERCA GREGARIA
DESERT LOCUST

LOCUSTA MIGRATORIA
AFRICAN MIGRATORY
LOCUST
(gregarious/migratory
phase)

SILIQUOFERA GRANDIS

ARCYPTERA FUSCA

LOCUSTA MIGRATORIA
AFRICAN MIGRATORY LOCUST
(solitary phase)

GRYLLUS CAMPESTRIS
FIELD CRICKET

Díd you know...

*The ability of the **Desert Locust** to destroy a whole crop of corn with astonishing speed has been known since Biblical times – a plague of locusts was one of the seven plagues to hit Ancient Egypt. The Desert Locust is gigantic, about 75 mm long.*

*The **Acrida mediterranea** is a grasshopper with a cone-shaped head and tapering legs. The female is up to 75 mm long. It does not 'sing' and lives in warm, damp plains of southern Europe.*

*The **Redwinged Grasshopper** is a species with red rear wings. It prefers dry places.*

*The sound of the **Arcyptera Fusca** is high-pitched and consists of many short notes followed by a burst of three seconds. It lives in the mountain pastures of the Alps and the Pyrenees. The male insect flies, but the female does not.*

*The **Acridoxena Hewaniana**, (Bush Cricket) has wings looking like small, curled-up leaves. It is an excellent example of an insect which can mimic its surroundings.*

*In some parts of Africa, people eat **locusts**. As a food, they are a good source of protein.*

*A swarm of **locusts** can cover an area of over 1000 square kilometres and eat up to 20,000 tonnes of food per day.*

FIELD CRICKET

Mouth: chewing

Movements: rarely jumps, prefers to fly and to run

Metamorphosis: incomplete

Length of adult: 3 cm

The Field Cricket belongs to the order of **Orthoptera** of insects and is found all over the world.

It is sometimes called the 'singing cricket' because of the loud, continuous sound it makes by lifting its front wings and rubbing one against the other. The sound is clearly heard, especially on warm, summer nights, but it is difficult to see the Field Cricket at close range.

It is very timid and at the slightest sign of anything strange, it will quickly flee into its underground lair. This can be up to half a metre deep, ending in a round chamber which is the actual nest. In front of the entrance to the lair, the cricket prepares a clean area where it sings to attract the female and to mark its territory. The female Field Cricket lays between 20 and 60 eggs during the autumn months. Young crickets are called 'nymphs' and they hatch in the spring. They shed their skins up to twelve times as they grow into adult crickets. Not all crickets sing. Some spend almost their whole lives underground. Others live in ant-hills, in symbiosis (helping and receiving help) with ants.

Although the cricket is related to the grasshopper and has hind legs ideal for jumping, it is not a great jumper and prefers to fly or to run rapidly over the ground. It eats leaves and small insects.

AFRICAN MIGRATORY LOCUST

The locust belongs to the **Orthoptera** order of insects. It is a species of grasshopper, and it can be found almost all over the world. From Biblical times, the African Migratory Locust has been known to cause serious damage to crops. But not all types of locusts are harmful. They are insects which usually live alone in what is called their 'solitary phase'. It is only when they congregate in thousands that they pose a danger. Then, under the influence of so many others, each locust changes its food, its size growing up to 70 mm long, and also its colour (yellow or mauve), becomes less bright. This is known as the 'gregarious phase'.

The locust eats mostly grasses; so, when thousands get together, no crops can stay undamaged. Also, eggs laid by a solitary female locust will spread about as they fall. But with many locusts all together, eggs will fall in a compact mass.

When the larvae hatch, they begin to group together in search of food - and once they reach the adult stage, they take to flight in swarms, swooping down on a field of crops and destroying it in a few hours.

Mouth: chewing

Movements: jumps, flies; migrates long distances

Speed: 10-25 km per hour

Metamorphosis: incomplete

Length of adult: 5 cm

PRAYING MANTIS

Mantids belong to one of the higher order of insects. There are more than 200 species of mantids, all related to the grasshopper, to the leaf-insect and the stick-insect.

The Praying Mantis gets its name because of its pose as if in prayer, with 'hands together', when it is still, waiting to trap another insect. Then, with a sudden stretch of its front legs, the Praying Mantis catches its victim, holding it between two rows of sharp points then taking it to the mouth to be eaten.

The reproduction of the Praying Mantis is also very strange. Whilst male and female are in the act of mating, the female grasps the head of the male and begins to eat him, even before mating is finished.

As well as insects, a large Praying Mantis will even eat lizards, small frogs and birds. By doing this, the female will take in a sufficient amount of protein to hatch a lot of eggs – up to 200 in a sort of cocoon called an ootheca. The female makes the ootheca from a sort of foam and this soon hardens, becoming like parchment.

Mouth: chewing

Development: Metamorphosis: incomplete; larvae moult 6-12 times before reaching adult stage

Length of adult: 7-8 cm

This opens in the spring-time, having survived even very low winter temperatures. Most species of mantid spend the winter in the egg phase. The first moulting of the larvae happens with the splitting of the membrane in which it has been enclosed from birth. Even then, although it is still immature, the larva already has front legs with which it can catch its first tiny, little prey.

There are over 2,000 species of mantids. Most are found in tropical regions throughout the world, but some species are found further north, in Mediterranean countries.

Some mantids from Africa and South-east Asia are highly coloured, looking exactly like a flower or a leaf. European mantids can also blend in perfectly with the leaves among which they hide to attack their victims.

The Chinese Mantid originates in eastern Asia, but it is also the largest mantid found in North America, measuring up to 10 cm long.

Did you know...

The **Hymenopus coronatus** (Orchid Mantis) is a very beautiful species which comes from Java. Its vivid colouring simulates the shadow and the streaks of the flowers among which it lives. During moulting it can change colour, according to the flowers surrounding it.

The **Empusa pennata** (Horned Praying Mantis) is easily recognized by its long neck. It can be green or mauve and spends all winter in the larva phase. Generally, this is recognisable, because, only at this stage of development, the mantid keeps the abdomen folded up above the thorax.

Most **mantids** (see photograph) are generally bad fliers. Desert species have no wings, and so they do not fly. But they are excellent runners.

The **Idolum Diabolicum** (African Devil Mantis) is one of the largest in the world. It blends in so perfectly with flowers that it is very difficult to see. It hangs on a plant with its head down and the bumps which cover its front part become easily mistaken for the tiny insects intent on eating the 'flower'.

Among the most curious of mantids are the **Acanthus falcate** found in Brazil, the **Pseudocreobotra Wahlbergi** (African Flower Mantid) and the **Gonylus Gongyloides** (Wandering Violin) from South-east Asia.

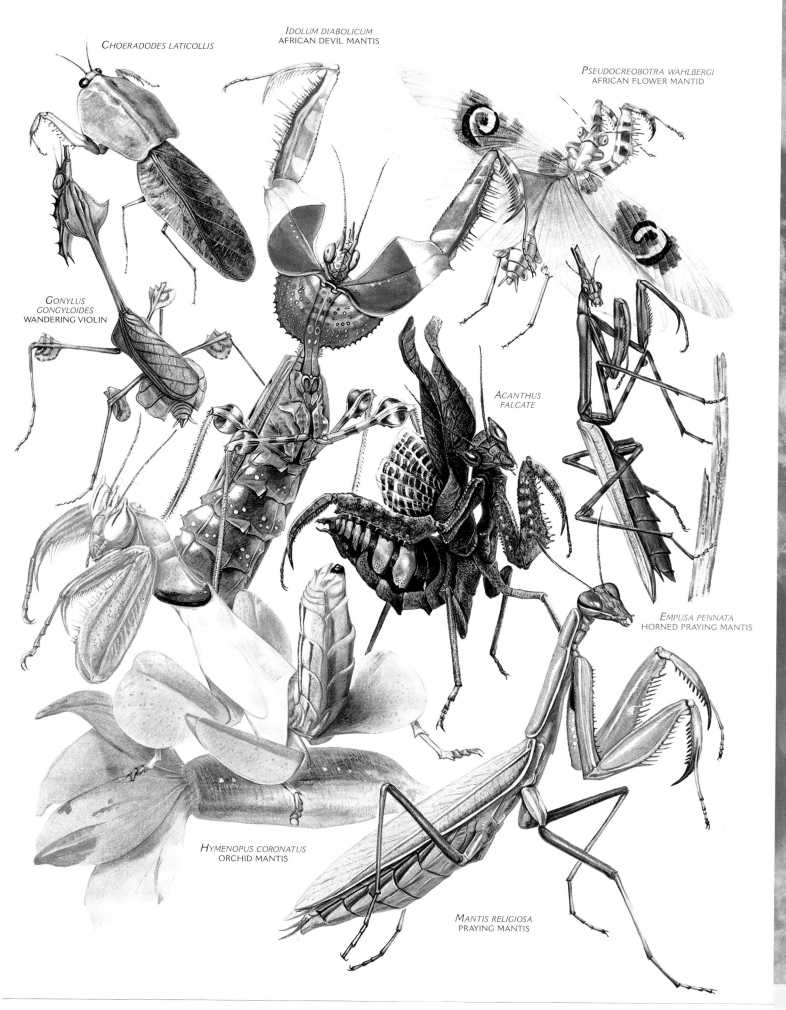

CHOERADODES LATICOLLIS

IDOLUM DIABOLICUM
AFRICAN DEVIL MANTIS

PSEUDOCREOBOTRA WAHLBERGI
AFRICAN FLOWER MANTID

GONYLUS
GONGYLOIDES
WANDERING VIOLIN

ACANTHUS
FALCATE

EMPUSA PENNATA
HORNED PRAYING MANTIS

HYMENOPUS CORONATUS
ORCHID MANTIS

MANTIS RELIGIOSA
PRAYING MANTIS

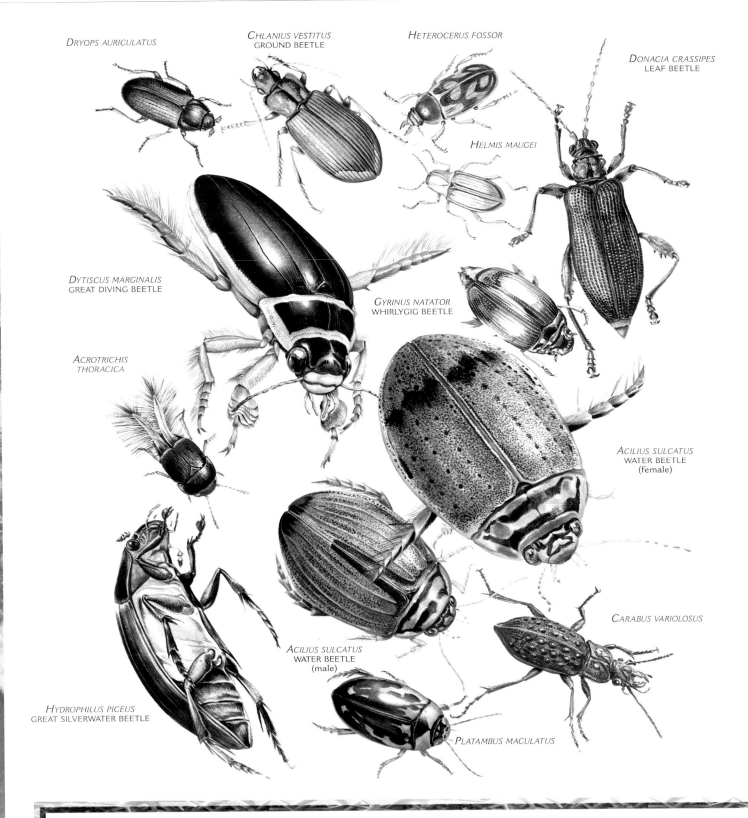

DRYOPS AURICULATUS

CHLANIUS VESTITUS
GROUND BEETLE

HETEROCERUS FOSSOR

DONACIA CRASSIPES
LEAF BEETLE

HELMIS MAUGEI

DYTISCUS MARGINALIS
GREAT DIVING BEETLE

GYRINUS NATATOR
WHIRLYGIG BEETLE

ACROTRICHIS
THORACICA

ACILIUS SULCATUS
WATER BEETLE
(female)

ACILIUS SULCATUS
WATER BEETLE
(male)

CARABUS VARIOLOSUS

HYDROPHILUS PICEUS
GREAT SILVERWATER BEETLE

PLATAMBUS MACULATUS

Díd you know...

There are many thousands of species of water beetles, all belonging to the insect order Coleoptera. The beetle, **Platambus maculates**, is a predator which lives mostly in flowing water.

The larvae of the **Dytiscus Marginalis** ('water tiger') pierces and sucks its prey until it is dry. The slow-moving adult is a water carnivore.

The **donacia crassipes** (leaf beetle) lays its eggs in the submerged stems of water plants. Their larvae never leave the bottom of ponds.

The female **Water Cockroach** fixes her cocoon containing her eggs beneath a leaf near the surface of the water.

The **Elater sanguineus** is one of the most brilliantly coloured coleoptera. It is a very rare species which feeds on dead and decomposing wood, especially the wood of the conifer.

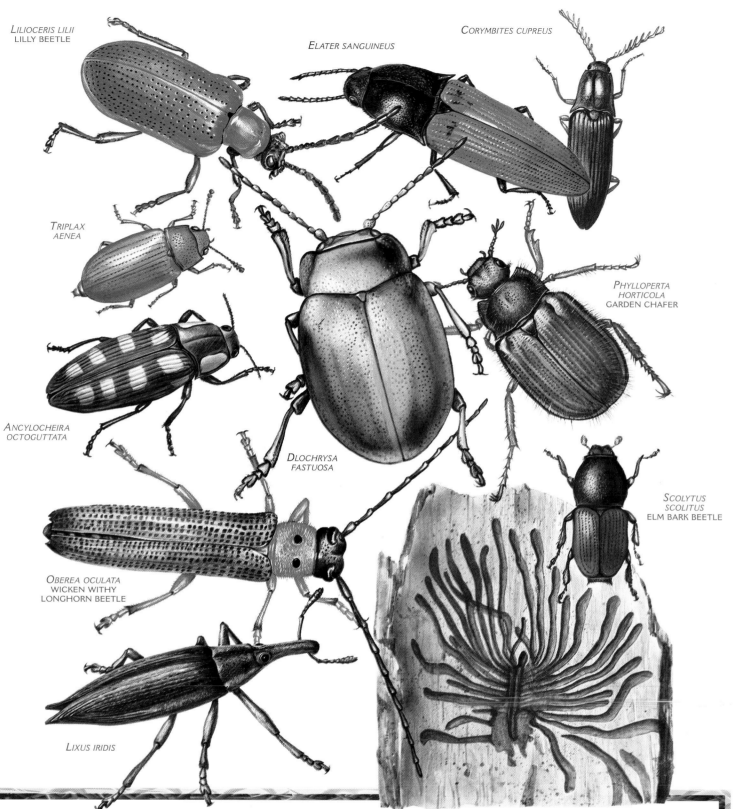

LILIOCERIS LILII
LILLY BEETLE

ELATER SANGUINEUS

CORYMBITES CUPREUS

TRIPLAX
AENEA

PHYLLOPERTA
HORTICOLA
GARDEN CHAFER

ANCYLOCHEIRA
OCTOGUTTATA

DLOCHRYSA
FASTUOSA

SCOLYTUS
SCOLITUS
ELM BARK BEETLE

OBEREA OCULATA
WICKEN WITHY
LONGHORN BEETLE

LIXUS IRIDIS

The **Lilly Beetle** belongs to the **Chrysomelidea** family, coleoptera characterized by bright colours and metal-like effects.

The **Elm Bark Beetle** digs long galleries beneath the bark of elm trees, seriously weakening the structure. Many species of coleoptera, commonly called **woodworm**, attack wood in our homes and in buildings.

To the Ancient Egyptians, the **Scarab Beetle** was a holy symbol of the sun.

Coleoptera belonging to the genus **Lixus**, are wood-boring weevils. All are members of the family of Curculionidae. They are easily recognized by the rigid proboscis (nose tube) on which angular antennae are attached.

The **Phyllopertha orticola** belongs to the important family of Scarabaeidae of which there are at least 30,000 species, all feeding on plants.

HORNET

The common European hornet belongs to the insect order of Hymenoptera. It is a larger species of the common wasp and so much more harmful. Its sting is very painful and the large quantity of poison it injects can even be dangerous. Its appearance is also quite fearsome – its yellow-black stripes are always seen as a sign of danger.

The hornet lives in country areas and lives near farmland and orchards. It feeds on ripe fruit, on the sap of plants and on other insects. The hornet is a sociable insect, which means it lives with others. A hornets' nest can be found hanging in barns or under the roofs of haylofts – although there are hornets which nest inside the holes of tree-trunks. One nest can hold up to a hundred of sterile workers as well as the powerful queen, the founder of the whole colony.

To build the nest, the hornet patiently chews pieces of rotten wood until it all becomes a type of papier mâché, ideal for building the walls and the tunnels, which are laid out horizontally. Towards the end of summer a few males from the colony fertilize those females which are fertile. The following spring, after having spent the winter sheltering from the cold, the queens who have survived leave the nest and go and find new colonies. Parent females provide insects to feed their larvae – but, like all wasps, the adult insect feeds on nectar.

Mouth: mixed, chewing and sucking

Metamorphosis: complete

Length of adult: 2-3 cm

Wing-span: 3-4 cm

Speed in flight: 6 metres per second – 2.6 km/h

Did you know...

*The society of **bees** is one of the most complex among those of insects. The worker bees feed the larvae and the queen with the royal jelly secreted in their glands. They collect pollen with which they produce honey, build honeycombs of wax and take care of the hive. When it gets too hot, the workers begin to move their wings all together to lower the temperature. Little by little, as the air cools, it condenses into drops of water to refresh the atmosphere and make the hive more comfortable.*

*Nests of **bumblebees** are made of moss and blades of grass, and here certain types of giant ants sometimes lay their eggs. This can result in the death of the queen bee, because the parasitic insects will destroy her eggs and overwhelm the nest with their own young. The bumblebee workers are not able to recognize the difference and raise the intruders' larvae as if they were those of the bumblebee.*

*The prey of the **Hunter Wasp** becomes paralysed by its poison, but without being killed.*

*The nest of the **Fowl Mite** is made of little balls of mud and contains just one larvae cell. This solitary insect lays just one egg.*

SPIDER WASP

Teeth: mixed, chewing and sucking

Metamorphosis: complete

Length of adult: up to 8 cm

Wing-span: 8-10 cm

Spider Wasps are just one species in the genus *Pepsis*. They are large, solitary predators and they live in some regions of South America, sometimes as far north as Mexico.

Taking their size into account – with its wing-span up to 10 cm – it comes as no surprise that a Spider Wasp can even attack large frogs although it feeds mainly on spiders, hence its name.

When a Spider Wasp comes across prey, it advances slowly, keeping on the ground a short distance away from its victim and with its wings by its side. It attempts to paralyse a frog by stinging it again and again. These attacks can last up to 50 minutes. At a certain point the poison takes effect and paralyses the victim which, still alive, is then taken down into the lair of the Spider Wasp. Here, it becomes a rich reserve of food for the larvae.

SCOLIA PROCER
SCOLID WASP

VESPA CRABRO
HORNET

BOMBUS TERRESTRIS
BUMBLEBEE

MUTILLA EUROPAEA
VELVET ANT

EUCHROREUS PURPURATUS
(male)

STILBUM CYANURUM
CUCKOO WASP

PEPSIS
TARANTULA HAWK
SPIDER WASP

*EUCHROREUS
PURPURATUS*
(female)

*EUMENES
COARCTATA*
FOWL MITE

AMMOPHILA SABULOSA
HUNTER WASP

*DINOPONERA
GIGANTEA*

17

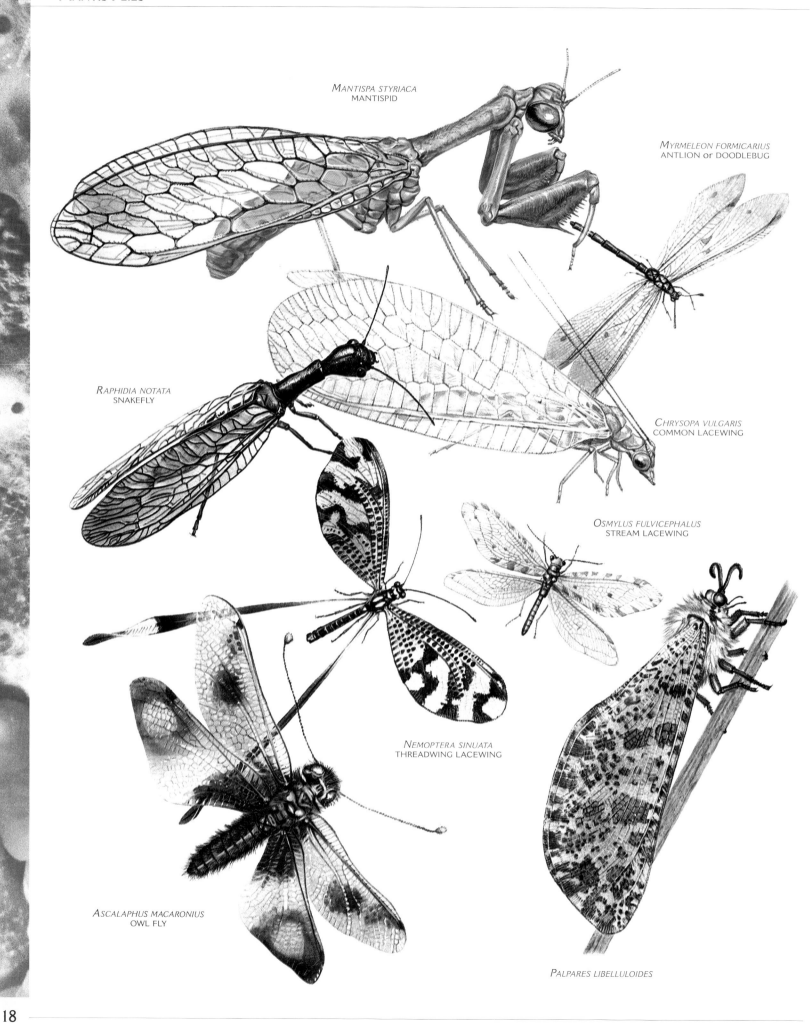

MANTISPA STYRIACA
MANTISPID

MYRMELEON FORMICARIUS
ANTLION or DOODLEBUG

RAPHIDIA NOTATA
SNAKEFLY

CHRYSOPA VULGARIS
COMMON LACEWING

OSMYLUS FULVICEPHALUS
STREAM LACEWING

NEMOPTERA SINUATA
THREADWING LACEWING

ASCALAPHUS MACARONIUS
OWL FLY

PALPARES LIBELLULOIDES

LACEWING

Mouth: chewing

Metamorphosis: complete

Length: about 1 cm

Lacewings belong to the insect order of Neuroptera. There are two families of Lacewing – the Green Lacewing and the Brown Lacewing. They are pale-coloured insects and have very delicate wings which are covered with a mesh of veins, making them look rather like lace. A Lacewing does not fly very well and is mainly nocturnal, spending the daylight hours among plants and appearing on lighted windows in the evening. When the time comes for the female Green Lacewing to lay eggs, she will produce long, delicate threads from her body which she fixes to the underside of a leaf and then lays one egg at the top of each thread. The Brown Lacewing is smaller then the Green Lacewing, and the female does not produce threads for her eggs.

Lacewings are welcome in gardens and farmlands because both the adult insects and their larvae feed on enormous quantities of the aphids which eat away at plants. The lacewing uses its curved, hollow jaws to suck the fluid from the body of an aphid until it is completely dry. The larvae of some lacewings then cover themselves with the dry skin of their aphid victims, using this as a disguise to help them surprise more prey and as protection against enemies.

Did you know...

The larvae of the **Palpares Libelluloides**, the largest antlion in Europe, shelters underneath the sand. Here it catches every type of insect in its large jaws, taking its prey under the sand and sucking out the body liquids. The Palpares Libelluloides flies mainly at night. Like all antlions, it likes dry, sandy surroundings.

The larvae of the **Mantispid** grow as parasites in the cocoons of eggs of various frogs. It looks like a little mantid but it is more slender and has lacy wings, like the lacewing. It feeds on little flies and flies both by day and night.

To protect against bad weather, the **Owl Fly** holds its wings rather like an awning above its body. Its appearance means that it is often mistaken for a butterfly. It has longer antennae than those of an antlion and flies more quickly.

The **Snakefly** gets its name because it has a very long thorax in proportion to the rest of its body. Its total body length is about 1 – 2 cm. The Snakefly is found in every continent except Australia. It is popular with farmers and growers, as well as town-dwellers, because it destroys the larvae of insects.

The **Nemoptera Sinuata** has very long rear wings. The male has a pair of glands in his abdomen which give off an unpleasant smell.

ANTLION OR DOODLEBUG

Mouth: chewing

Metamorphosis: complete

Length: 20-25 mm

An antlion looks rather like a dragonfly, except that it has much larger antennae. Its larvae are fierce predators of ants and other insects which live on the ground. The larvae of some antlions dig small, tunnel-like holes in sand, where they bury themselves, except for their jaws. When ants or other prey fall to the bottom of

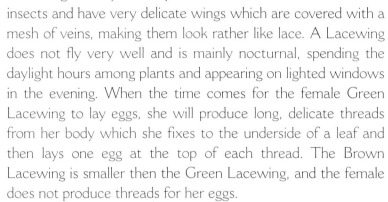

this little pit, the antlion larvae eat them. The adult antlion does not feed and so the larva must eat enough food to keep it alive once it becomes adult. Once it has done this, the larva makes a cocoon of silk, which it spins itself, and sand. When the adult insect emerges from the cocoon, it is ready to mate and so begin the life-cycle again.

Although antlions are most common in central-southern Europe they can be found in most parts of the continent, including southern Scandinavia. They are also common in North America and in the United States, where they are called doodlebugs.

COMMON MOSQUITO

Mouth: sucking

Metamorphosis: complete

Length: 8-13 cm

Life of Adult: 3-5 days

The common mosquito can be found almost anywhere in the world. It is harmless but very irritating. Normally, it sucks the blood only of birds and humans. Its abdomen is rather wide and covered in scales. The female's antennae are short; in the male, the antennae are long and feathery, so that the insect can collect the nectar on which it feeds. The male's antennae are also used to sense the high-pitched humming sounds made by the female and to recognize the presence of other mosquitoes. Both male and female have a long, hollow proboscis through which they suck their food. The common mosquito lays its eggs in all types of stagnant water.

To breathe, the larvae positions itself vertically below the skin of the water, so that the bottom part of its body, where the respiratory organs are, is above the surface. The larvae feed on animal and vegetable matter, but the males of many species of mosquito 'fast' for the whole of their brief lives and survive by using up the reserves of food taken in during the larva stage. The female lives much longer than the male.

GARDEN MOSQUITO

Mouth: sucking

Metamorphosis: complete

Wingspan: 10 cm in the largest examples

The Garden Mosquito can be found almost all over the world. It is mostly noctural and looks very much like a giant mosquito, although it does not bite or sting.

The Garden Mosquito lives almost wholly in fields. It is quite lazy and, right from the start of its brief life, prefers to spend its time among the grass, always flying just above the surface of the ground in a clumsy, heavy sort of flight.

The adult feeds on nectar and other vegetable juices. But the long, soft larvae are very harmful because they feed only on the roots of vegetables, especially carrots. They are very resistant to pesticides and farmers see them as a pest and a danger.

Like all mosquitoes, the Garden Mosquito needs water. The female lays her eggs on muddy or moist surfaces, and as rain falls, so the larvae hatch. When the land is uncultivated, the larvae satisfy themselves with the roots of grasses.

Did you know...

Unlike all other flying insects, those which belong to the **Diptera** class have only one pair of true wings. The hind wings are in the form of 'halteres' – tiny, little fin-like organs which enables the insect to keep its balance during flight. In many of the larger insects in this class, the halteres are covered with scales.

The male and female of **Bibio Hortulanus** (Mark's Fly) are quite different to each other; the female has a more narrow head and smaller eyes. They live particularly near trees, and close to farms and gardens where they attack the roots of plants.

The adult male of the **Anopheles Mosquito** (see larvae in photograph) is easily recognized by its feelers, which look like little golf clubs. It is the female which carries malaria, and she, too, has long feelers. In a resting position, the adult keeps the abdomen leaning towards the surface on which it has landed, whereas the mosquito larvae lie horizontally on the surface of the water.

The female of the **Black Fly** sucks the blood of many mammals, injecting them with a poisonous substance with her saliva.

The female **Sand Fly** carries the germs which can cause serious illnesses in humans, for example, a tropical disease called Pappataci Fever.

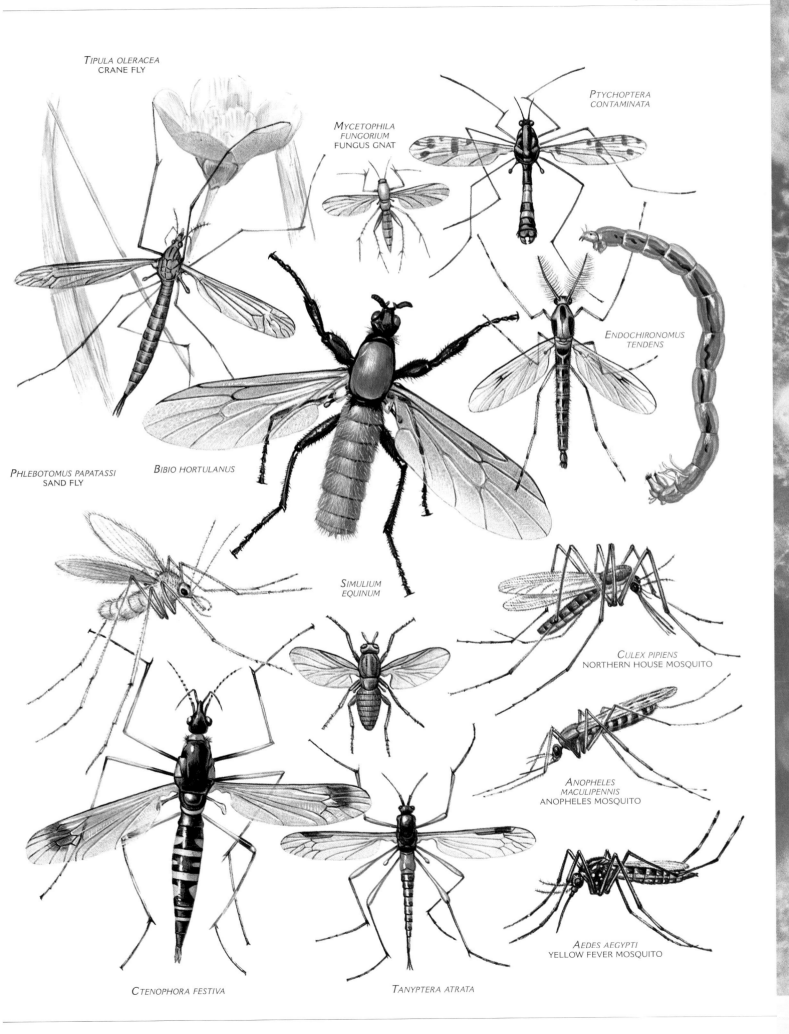

TIPULA OLERACEA
CRANE FLY

MYCETOPHILA
FUNGORIUM
FUNGUS GNAT

PTYCHOPTERA
CONTAMINATA

ENDOCHIRONOMUS
TENDENS

PHLEBOTOMUS PAPATASSI
SAND FLY

BIBIO HORTULANUS

SIMULIUM
EQUINUM

CULEX PIPIENS
NORTHERN HOUSE MOSQUITO

ANOPHELES
MACULIPENNIS
ANOPHELES MOSQUITO

AEDES AEGYPTI
YELLOW FEVER MOSQUITO

CTENOPHORA FESTIVA

TANYPTERA ATRATA

TSETSE FLY

Mouth: sucking

Metamorphosis: complete

Length of adult: 10-13 mm

The Tsetse Fly may look harmless, but it is the carrier of terrible disease which can strike many species of animals, including all domestic animals, as well as humans. It lives mainly in Africa in the southern region of the Sahara Desert.

It feeds by breaking the skin of its victim with its beak-like mouth then sucking the blood. Unlike the horsefly and the mosquito, where only the female feeds on blood, in the Tsetse Fly, both sexes are 'blood-suckers'.

So far, twenty similar species have been discovered, some living in the open spaces of desert and jungle regions, others among thick vegetation.

When it comes to reproduction, instead of laying a certain quantity of eggs, the female Tsetse Fly produces only one which she carries inside her body. Here, the larva develops, nourished by a food which the female produces by special glands, having sucked enough blood for the development of the egg. As the larva develops, it breathes through two ducts which develop from a swelling on the female's body.

FRUIT FLY

Mouth: sucking

Metamorphosis: complete

Length: 4.5-5 mm

There are many species of Fruit Fly, all seen as serious pests to fruit farmers. The Mediterranean Fruit Fly is common in the USA and most of Europe. It has grey-red wings, spotted with black at the bottom. The thorax is black with spots and covered with a fine silver down. After mating, the female will use a type of sting to break open the ripened skin of citrus fruits such as oranges and grapefruit, then lay her eggs inside. Some are killed by the oils in the skin of certain types of citrus fruits, but with up to 500 eggs laid, some are bound to survive. Once hatched, the larvae feed on the flesh of the fruit. In the case of the Apple Fruit Fly, the larva will eat the flesh to the core, so the fruit goes rotten and then falls. The Fruit Fly was identified in Malaysia at the beginning of the 18th century. After that, it invaded all hot and temperate countries in the world. In the USA, a 'war' is constantly being waged against all types of fruit flies, especially in Florida and in Hawaii. Crops are sprayed with pesticides during the mating season of the Fruit Fly, and there are strict quarantine laws to regulate all fruit imported from other countries. But, the Fruit Fly continues to survive.

Did you know...

The female of the **Tabanus Atratus** (Black Horse Fly) can suck up to 55 mg of blood with just one bite, attacking its victim near the eyes. But the male Black Horse Fly feeds only on nectar and dew.

One of the names for the Devil is Beelzebub, which means 'Lord of the Flies' – and the ugly appearance of the **fly** does make many of us to think of this insect as a 'devilish' creature, especially when we know the fly to be a tireless pursuer which is able to feed on rubbish. In addition, flies can cause illness and disease, and are virtually indestructible.

The **Killer Shore Fly** from North America has front legs similar to the Praying Mantis.

The larvae of both the **Warble Fly** and the **Cattle Fly** develop beneath the skin of cattle. This causes painful lumps which have to be lanced.

Flies belonging to the **Diosophilidae** family and especially the **Vinegar Fly** were first studied by an American biologist in 1900. It was soon discovered that they can be easily bred and reproduce very quickly, which is why these insects have since become important in the study of the heredity of characteristics in human beings. In addition, the Vinegar Fly has only four pairs of chromosomes in the protein molecule nucleus of a cell, and this feature makes research into the DNA which carries hereditary information much easier.

BRAULA COECA
BEE LOUISE

OCYPTERA BRASSICARIA

ASILUS CRABRONIFORMIS
ROBBER FLY

OCHTERA MANTIS
KILLER SHORE FLY

CERATITIS CAPITATA
MEDITERRANEAN FRUIT
FLY

LUCILIA CAESAR
GREEN BOTTLE

CHRYSOPS CAECUTIENS
HORSE FLY

GLOSSINA PALPALIS
TSETSE FLY

CONOPS QUADRIFASCIATUS
WASP FLY

HYPODERMA BOVIS
WARBLE FLY

CYRTUS GIBBUS

CELYPHUS

LIMPET

A limpet is a marine snail, a crustacean belonging to the order of cirripedes. There are many types, each with a shell which is similar to that of a mollusc. A limpet fixes itself to underwater surfaces or any submerged object, even to the shell of a marine turtle, with only

Reproduction: Hermaphrodite

Habitat: sea

Life-style: attached by the base

Length: 8-10 cm

the legs protruding from the shell.

It takes in water through the abdomen in order to filter the tiny organisms of plankton on which it feeds. Indeed, some limpets survive only on the water trapped inside their shells. Limpets detach themselves only to feed on seaweed, always going back to the same spot.

Limpets are found in the Atlantic and the Pacific Oceans. They are a danger to shipping, because, in great numbers, they weigh down the keel (or spine) of the ship and cause damage.

GIANT MUSSEL SHRIMP

Reproduction: separate sexes

Habitat: open seas at depths of 1000-3000 m

Life-style: part of plankton

Length: 25 mm

Despite its name, the Giant Mussel Shrimp is a tiny crustacean, only 25 mm long - but, compared to other mussel shrimps which are no longer than 1 mm, it is a true 'giant'. It lives in the Pacific, at depths of up to 2000 m.

All mussel shrimps have an hard covering called a carapace in the form of two valves which are joined on the back. Unlike other crustaceans, a mussel shrimp has only two or three pairs of tiny feet. But it has two pairs of antennae which are highly developed and which it uses like oars as it swims.

Those species of mussel shrimp which crawl along the sea bed use the appendages of the thorax as limbs and the last pair act as a sort of sweeper to clean mud from the inside of the shell.

Some mussel shrimps are blind. Some have a central eye. Others have a pair of simple or compound eyes like those of insects. Sexes are separate in marine species, whilst in the freshwater species there are no sexes and reproduction is by parthenogenesis – which means, without fertilization.

Over 10,000 extinct species of mussel shrimps have been identified, some dating back to over 500 million years ago.

Did you know...

The **Water Flea** or **Daphnia** is a tiny crustacean, only 3 – 5 mm long, with a thin, transparent shell and which lives in pools of fresh water. To move, it does not use its legs, which are enclosed in its shell, but its long antennae. Its diet is mainly tiny fish and other minute water creatures.

The **Fairy Shrimp** and the **Brine Shrimp** are two branchiopods – freshwater crustaceans. The Brine Shrimp lives in salt water and the salt water lakes of temperate zones. If it becomes immersed in a quantity of salt, it changes colour.

The **Tadpole Shrimp** is a branchiopod which is virtually the same today as its ancestors of at least 200 million years ago – and as we know from fossil remains which have been found. It gets its name from its oval-shaped hard covering and a long tail, so that it looks like a tadpole. It is about 10 cm long.

Another branchiopod is the **Branchipus Stagnalis**, only 23 mm long.

The maximum length of the **Limnadia Lenticularis** is 17 mm. It moves lazily on the bottom of pools of fresh water which form in summer time.

The **Rock Crab** forms part of plankton. It is sometimes called the **Peacock Rock Crab** because of its spread of feathery appendages which look like a peacock's tail.

Barnacles are Cirripede crustaceans which support themselves by tubular, flexible 'feet' about 10 cm long.

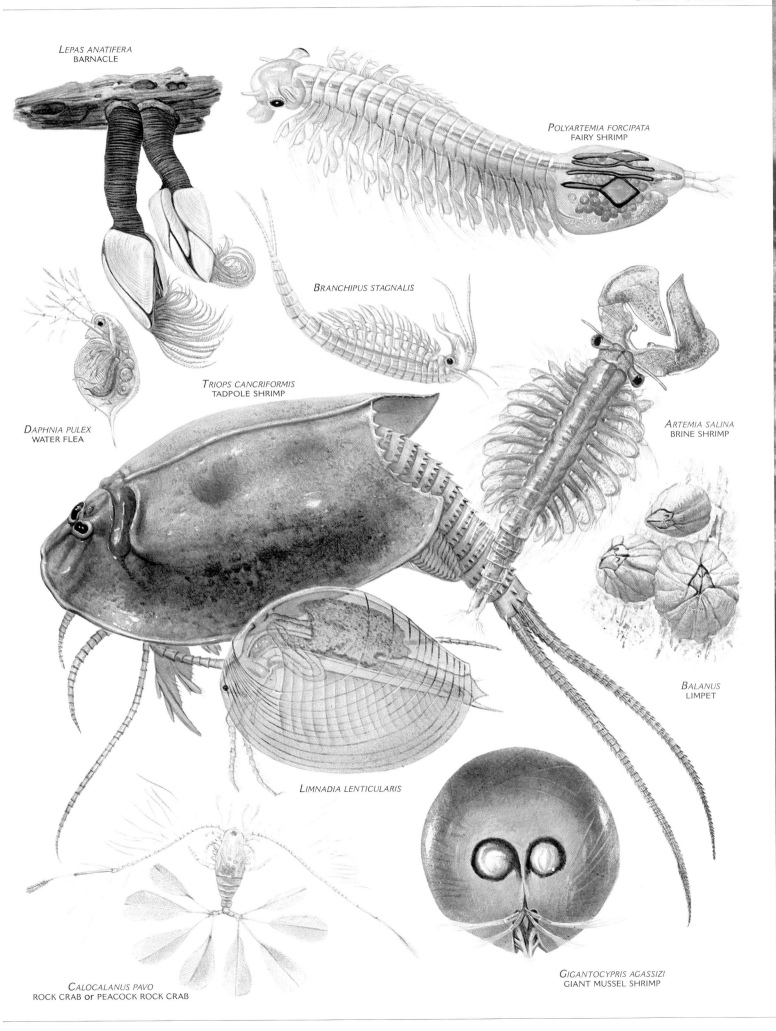

LEPAS ANATIFERA
BARNACLE

POLYARTEMIA FORCIPATA
FAIRY SHRIMP

BRANCHIPUS STAGNALIS

TRIOPS CANCRIFORMIS
TADPOLE SHRIMP

ARTEMIA SALINA
BRINE SHRIMP

DAPHNIA PULEX
WATER FLEA

BALANUS
LIMPET

LIMNADIA LENTICULARIS

CALOCALANUS PAVO
ROCK CRAB **or** PEACOCK ROCK CRAB

GIGANTOCYPRIS AGASSIZI
GIANT MUSSEL SHRIMP

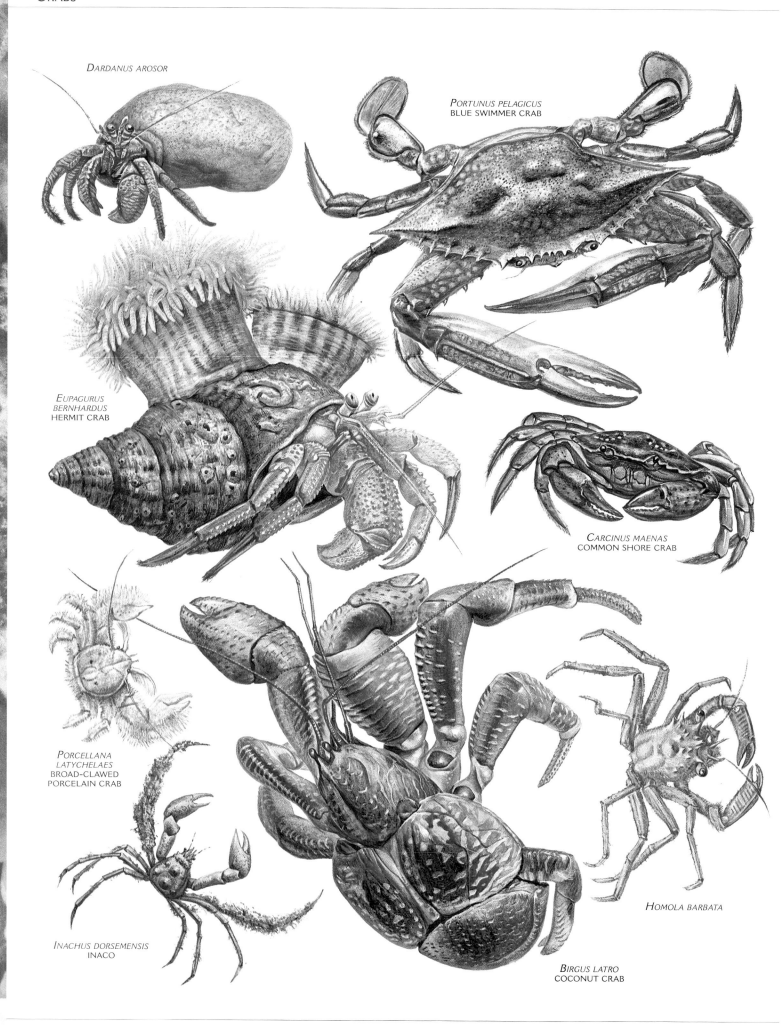

DARDANUS AROSOR

PORTUNUS PELAGICUS
BLUE SWIMMER CRAB

EUPAGURUS BERNHARDUS
HERMIT CRAB

CARCINUS MAENAS
COMMON SHORE CRAB

PORCELLANA LATYCHELAES
BROAD-CLAWED PORCELAIN CRAB

HOMOLA BARBATA

INACHUS DORSEMENSIS
INACO

BIRGUS LATRO
COCONUT CRAB

COMMON SHORE CRAB

Habitat: the coast

Region found: Mediterranean

Length of carapace: 4-5 cm

Like all crabs, the Common Shore Crab belongs to the class Decapoda. It can be found along all European coastlines. At the least sign of danger, it runs and hides itself with its typical sideways movement.

The carapace (rigid plating) is black-green, rather like marble to look at, and its pincers are most clearly seen at the tip. At the front of its body, the Common Shore Crab

has three triangular teeth, set between its eyes which are on stalks. This crab is well used to ever-changing surroundings, which is why it is so easily found in harbours. It will eat anything, from small fish to shrimps and worms.

It is very aggressive and never lives with smaller crabs, or those which are weak due to the time of sloughing (shedding the carapace plating when this becomes too small). It can often be seen ready to do battle, raising its pincers which are always open; if necessary, it can defend itself by using only one leg if the other is broken off. Then it grows this again by successive sloughing.

COCONUT CRAB

Habitat: coast

Region found: East Pacific

Length: up to 46 mm

Weight of adult: 2-2.5 kg

Coconut Crabs can be found all along the Eastern Pacific coast.

This crab is a large crustacean which gets its name because it is supposed to be able to make coconuts fall to the ground, break them open and then eat them – but this is only a story.

The favourite foods of the Coconut Crab are the remains of fish or rotting molluscs which it finds along the beach. Only rarely does it feed on the flesh of a coconut and then it has to find one which is already open. Despite the strength of its pincers, it would not be able to lift a coconut, let alone open it. But, because of this story, this crab is also called the Robber Crab.

This crab reproduces in the sea and its larvae live in water until they develop into adults; once adult, the Coconut Crab swims towards the land. Because it breathes in oxygen from the air, it does not need to go into water again. The adult grows to about 1 m from head to tail.

Did you know...

The **Eupagurus bernhardus** or Hermit Crab (see photograph) has a soft, frail body, which is why it lives in empty shells for protection. After each sloughing, its body grows, and so the Hermit Crab goes in search of a larger shell. It lives in symbiosis (each creature helping the other) with the sea anemone. This sea

creature feeds on the remains of the Hermit Crab's meals and in return protects the crab from enemies with its stinging appendages.

The **Dardanus arosor**, another type of hermit crab also shelters in empty mollusc shells and lives in symbiosis with the sea anemone.

The **crab Porcellana platychelaes** (Broad-Clawed Porcelain Crab), is a type of a hermit crab with a flat body – and so it goes

in search of flat shells, not spiral.

The **Portunus pelagicus** (Blue Swimmer Crab) and the **Inachus dorsemensis** (Inaco) are fairly common in Mediterranean waters. The **Homola barbata** lives in very deep waters.

It is easy to distinguish the female of the **Common Shore Crab** from the male by examining the abdomen; in the female, this is large, because it has to carry eggs, whilst the stomach of the male is narrow and triangular.

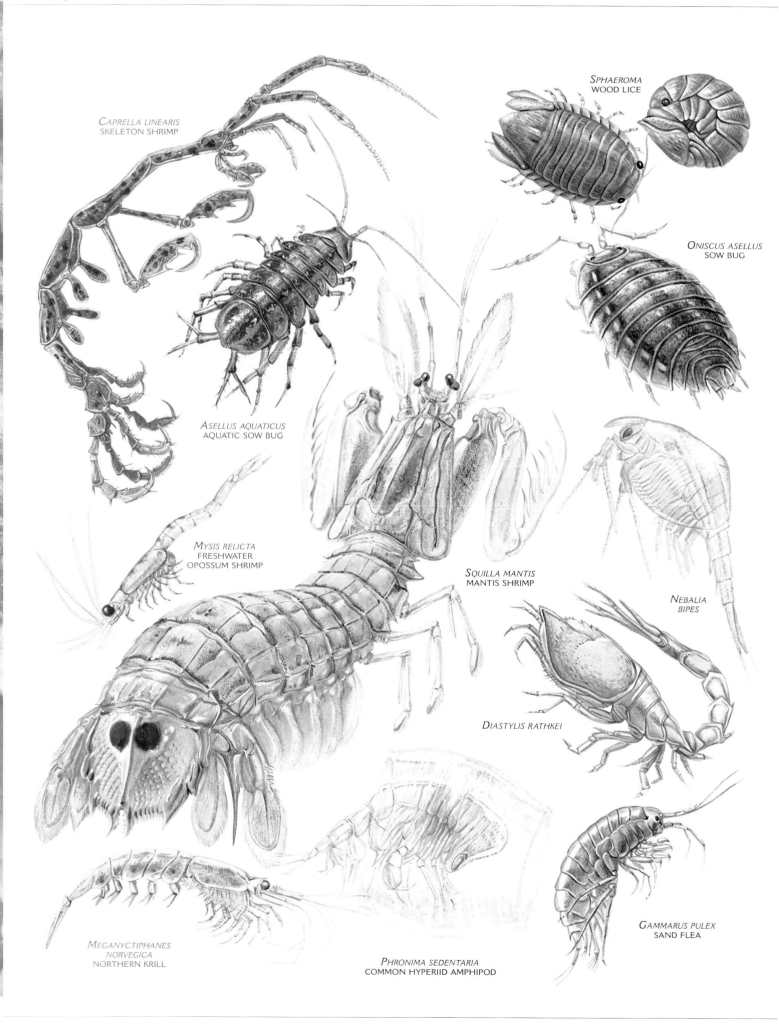

CAPRELLA LINEARIS
SKELETON SHRIMP

SPHAEROMA
WOOD LICE

ONISCUS ASELLUS
SOW BUG

ASELLUS AQUATICUS
AQUATIC SOW BUG

MYSIS RELICTA
FRESHWATER
OPOSSUM SHRIMP

SQUILLA MANTIS
MANTIS SHRIMP

NEBALIA
BIPES

DIASTYLIS RATHKEI

GAMMARUS PULEX
SAND FLEA

MEGANYCTIPHANES
NORVEGICA
NORTHERN KRILL

PHRONIMA SEDENTARIA
COMMON HYPERIID AMPHIPOD

KRILL

Habitat: cold oceans,
between the surface and depths of 600 m

Life-style: plankton

Average length: 5-7 cm

Krill comes from a Norwegian word and it is the name given to dozens of species of tiny crustaceans which together constitute the only food of whales. All Krill crustaceans are similar to tiny shrimps and they live in the cold waters of the oceans, near to the North Pole and the Antarctic continent. They lay their eggs at a depth of about 250 m, and as the larvae develop they gradually move up towards the surface, feeding on tiny little organisms as they go. The larvae take about two years to develop into adults.

Krill spend their lives in the open sea, being transported by the currents and feeding on plankton. In turn, they are part of a 'super-plankton' which in a mass can weigh hundreds of millions of tonnes. A shoal of krill is long-shaped, a mass of white or red. During the mating season, shoals of krill in the Antarctic Ocean can reach a density of 18 kg for each cubic metre of water. During summer in the southern hemisphere, whales can consume over 150 million tonnes of krill!

Did you know...

The **Skeleton Shrimp** looks rather like the Praying Mantis. It lives in the Atlantic and in the Mediterranean Sea. It swims elegantly, keeping its head down and its legs pointing up, so that its body is in the shape of a letter 'S'.

The **Common Hyperiid Amphipod** belongs to the same order of amphipoda as the Skeleton Shrimp and Sand Flea.

The **Sand Flea** is a small crustacean, only 20 mm long. It is very common on beaches and very useful because it feeds on plant matter and small animals and plant waste washed up on by the tide.

The **Aquatic Sow Bug** belongs to the same order as the land-dwelling sow bug. It lives among the plants in fresh, calm waters. It does not swim, but crawls slowly along. The female Aquatic Sow Bug carries her eggs and cares for her young until they can support themselves on their first four pairs of little legs.

The common **Mantis Shrimp** (see photograph right) of European seas is about 20 cm long. The female lays almost 50,000 eggs, which she carries between her front claws for about 10 weeks, giving up her search for food.

The **Freshwater Opossum Shrimp** is a small crustacean which lives in the freshwater lakes of northern Europe.

SOW BUG

The sow bug belongs to the order of Isopods. It is the only crustacean which has adapted to life on land, without needing water, unlike the shrimp or the crab to which it is related. There are many species of sow bug throughout the world, the largest no longer than a few centimetres.

Sow bugs are sociable creatures, which means that they live in groups. They tend to stay close together in order to reduce excessive perspiration, which is one of the risks of living on the land. They hide under stones, in rotted tree-trunks and all places where there is the warmth and the dark which they need. In sunlight or heat, a sow bug will die in a short time from de-hydration. Most sow bugs roll themselves into a ball to protect themselves from danger, like the pangolin and the armadillo. Their shell is very strong and protects them from attacks by frogs. Sow bugs also produce a bitter, evil-smelling liquid which keeps millipedes and ants away.

The sow bug is very similar to the pill bug, to which it is related. Like the pill bug, the sow bug is often called the wood louse. The adult sow bug grows to a length of 18 mm.

Habitat: warm grounds

Breathing: modified gills

Length: 2 cm

GLOSSARY

antennae – name given to an insect's feelers, usually on the head.

aphids – tiny insects which feed on plants. The most common aphid is the greenfly.

appendages – an appendage is usually a leg. It can, however, be anything which projects from the central part of the body of an animal, such as a leg, a wing or an antenna.

Arachnida – a class of creatures which includes scorpions and spiders. An arachnid has a segmented body divided into two parts. The front part has four pairs of legs, but no antennae.

carapace – the hard, rigid body covering of crustaceans and arachnids.

cephalothorax - the bodies of insects and some crustaceans are divided into three parts, head, thorax and abdomen. The cephalothorax is where the head and thorax are fused together.

chelicerae – pincer-like appendages nearest the mouth of arachnids and some crustaceans. The creature uses them to bite its prey and to inject poison into its victim. Spiders also use their chelicerae for spinning silk. Crabs use them to grip their prey.

chelicerates – animals with chelicerae.

cirripedes – crustaceans such as limpets and barnacles which swim about as larvae, but become almost permanently fixed to a surface when adult.

class – a broad category of animals which have some features in common. Many orders may make up one class.

Coleoptera – an order of insects which are beetles.

compound eyes – eyes which are made up of many lenses and so which can see in many directions at the same time. The human eye has only one lens.

Crustaceans – a class of mostly aquatic (water-dwelling), invertebrate animals with a horny or bony outer shell, a pair of appendages on each segment of the body and two pairs of antennae.

cuticle – a hard skin of varying thickness which protects the outside of many invertebrate animals.

decapod – a crustacean which has ten legs.

family – a group of animals which are closely related. There may be many genuses within a family, and many families within an order.

genus – one or more related species which form part of a family of animals.

gregarious phase – a phase in the life of some insects such as locusts, where it likes or needs to be in the company of others of its kind.

habitat – a creature's natural home.

hermaphrodite – an animal with the organs of both sexes, male and female.

Hymenoptera – an order of insects with four transparent wings, including pollinating insects such as bees and wasps.

invertebrate – without a backbone.

Isopoda – an order of crustaceans, each with a flat long body, a thorax of seven segments and an abdomen of six segments.

mantids – large, slow-moving insects which feed on other living insects.

mantle – the body cavity in molluscs and in crustaceans such as water fleas, the Fairy Shrimp and the Tadpole Shrimp.

metamorphosis – a complete transformation within the life-cycle of an animal, for example, a larva being transformed into a butterfly.

complete metamorphosis – comprises three stages of transformation, e.g. egg, larva, adult animal.

incomplete metamorphosis – comprises only two stages, with the egg hatching into an adult animal without going through the larva stage.

mites – tiny, arachnid parasites, living off plant material or other animals.

mollusc – a creature with a soft, compact body without an internal skeleton and which is sub-divided into a head and a trunk.

Neuroptera – a large order of insects which have four veined wings and include lacewings and snakeflies.

nocturnal – living by night and sleeping by day.

Opiliones – an order of insects with small bodies and very long, thread-like legs, such as the Daddy Long-Legs.

order – one section of a class, comprising animals which are quite closely related.

Orthoptera – order of insects with firm front wings and folded hind wings.

oviparous – egg-laying.

ovoviviparous – where fertilized eggs develop within the female body, but, unlike mammals, these are not nourished by her.

parasite – an animal which lives off another.

parthenogenesis – reproduction by a female without male fertilization.

pedipalps – second pair of appendages in arachnids. Sometimes these are used for chewing. sometimes as huge, powerful pincers and for gripping, as organs of reproduction and for tasting.

Pepsis – a genus of tarantula hawk spiders.

plankton – mass of drifting organisms in water.

predator – a hunter of prey.

proboscis – a trunk-like snout used for sucking up food.

Scarabaeidae – a family of beetles which form part of the order Coleoptera.

secreted – formed and hidden within the body.

Solifugae – sun spiders.

solitary phase – a phase in the lives of some insects where it prefers to be alone.

species – a special kind of animal. One or more species can make a genus.

spermatophore – a capsule containing fertile sperm and which some male arachnids deposit on the ground ready for the female to lay her eggs.

submerged – completely under water.

symbiosis – where two different species exist together, each one helping the other.

thorax – the part of the body of an insect or crustacean between the head and the abdomen.

tick – a microscopic parasite arachnid which feeds on the blood of whatever creature it lives on.

trachea – a tube within the body of air-breathing creatures.

vertebrate – with a backbone.

INDEX